A Inspector Calls

The A–Z to Surviving a
Tax Investigation

Daniel Dover
and
Tim Hindle

with cartoons by
Michael Heath

P
PROFILE BOOKS

First published in Great Britain in 1999 by
Profile Books Ltd
58A Hatton Garden
London EC1N 8LX
www.profilebooks.co.uk

Copyright © BDO Stoy Hayward, 1999
8 Baker Street
London W1M 1DA
www.bdo.co.uk

Typeset in Columbus by
Geoff Green Book Design
Printed in Great Britain by
St Edmundsbury Press, Bury St Edmunds

A CIP catalogue record for this book is available from the British Library.

ISBN 1 86197 143 5

Contents

DANIEL DOVER, a specialist in Inland Revenue
investigations, is a partner at BDO Stoy Hayward
in London.

TIM HINDLE is the author of several books on finance
and business and is a former finance editor of
The Economist. He was the founder editor of *EuroBusiness*
and has been editor of *Director* magazine.

MICHAEL HEATH is cartoons editor of *The Spectator*.

Acknowledgements

I am indebted to many people for their valuable contribution to this book.

To Stephen Davis, Peter Leach and Philip Rubenstein at BDO Stoy Hayward and Andrew Franklin at Profile who have helped, encouraged and cajoled throughout its production.

To Stuart Gerber, Frank Goldberg, Geoffrey Hollander, Shelley Kaufman, Richard Morley, Mark Sassoon and Mike Sutherland – the tax investigations team at BDO Stoy Hayward – for their diligence, dedication, teamwork, high standards and friendship.

Enormous thanks are also due to my wife, Helen, and 'the boys' who have been a constant support and have over the years endured the many unsocial hours spent with clients in trouble.

Finally, a word of thanks to the main protagonists of the tax investigation: to my current and former clients for the privilege of representing them, and to the Inland Revenue's Special Compliance Office, without whom…

Daniel Dover
BDO Stoy Hayward

Foreword

No-one likes paying tax.

Most people worry at some time or another about their tax returns and about keeping their financial affairs in order. But sometimes it can get worse. And if the Inland Revenue inspector is on your tail, it can be disruptive and distressing.

When the inspector calls, any one of a number of emotions is common. Reactions vary from denial that the matter might be serious, anger with the 'unjustness' of the revenue's claim – or just sheer terror at the thought of losing everything and ending up in prison. There are two pieces of advice that any experienced professional will give: first, don't panic and second, get expert help at the outset. You will need someone on your side who knows the jargon and understands how the Inland Revenue operates.

If you do receive the call, this book will give you a clearer idea of what lies ahead and how best to get through it. In the meantime, good luck – and get help.

is for Anxiety

When you know you've been caught

A letter in the post

It is a strange fact of life that the toughest, most aggressive people in business go wobbly all over when they receive a letter from the Inland Revenue's investigations arm, the Special Compliance Office (SCO), saying that their tax affairs are under investigation.

Many people panic at such times and begin to exhibit bizarre and totally irrational behaviour. They might start setting fire to small pieces of paper, for instance, or transferring assets into their mother-in-law's name.

A standard opening letter from the SCO looks like this:

Messrs BDO Stoy Hayward
8 Baker Street
LONDON W1M 1DA

Dear Sirs

I refer to your letter of   sent to   District.

Please note that this office will be responsible for future enquiries. Enquiries will now be conducted under Code of Practice 8 and I have attached two booklets and forms IR120 herewith which should be given to your clients.

Enquiries into your clients 1997/98 Self Assessment Returns have also now been formally opened under Section 9A Taxes Management Act 1970.

I would like to meet with your clients to discuss the company's and their own personal taxation affairs and suggest that a meeting take place at your offices at 10.00 am on Thursday   I would be grateful if you would telephone me to confirm the arrangements.

Yours faithfully

HM Inspector of Taxes

It will be sent either to your tax advisers or (if you don't have any) to you direct. It may sound bland. But don't be fooled. It is a very serious matter.

Sometimes investigations begin with a seemingly innocent letter from the taxpayer's local office making a seemingly innocent inquiry. The taxpayer, however, knows that it's the $64,000 question; the sort of question that makes you say to yourself: 'Oh xxxx, I've been caught' – or words to that effect.

With the introduction of self-assessment and the revenue's powers to spot-check taxpayers' returns, this type of approach is probably going to increase.

Gotcha

The feeling of being caught is something that successful entrepreneurs in particular are not well-equipped to cope with. People with enough income and assets for it to be worth the revenue's while to investigate their affairs tend to be in control of their lives. They are used to getting what they want.

They spend much of their time trying to find ways round obstacles. And they score points for doing so, and for doing it better than anyone else. A letter from the SCO in pursuit of a serious case of tax evasion undermines their sense of being in charge.

Moreover, it is something that is completely outside most people's experience, something that does not arise in their day-to-day dealings with other parts of the tax collecting system.

There is also the shame and embarrassment of it. Everyone in this world has skeletons they'd rather keep hidden in their cupboard. But once people are caught up in an investigation they realise that they might have to expose themselves and their innermost being. Not only to a professional adviser, but also to a government agency.

Gut reactions

For some, the experience is akin to being caught speeding at 100mph on the M40 in their Jag. Their first reaction is: 'How can I get out of this?'

Other common first reactions include:

- I'm finished.
- Am I going to Ford (open prison)?
- Can I just go bankrupt?
- I need Prozac.
- Can they extradite me?
- Will 'she' find out?
- Is my phone being tapped?
- Are 'they' following me?
- Why have they picked on me?

A cool and early analysis of the extent of the problem is the key to a successful conclusion. And that can only be done with the help of experienced professionals. It cannot be done by the person you played 18 holes of golf with last Sunday, nor by a man you met on the plane coming back from Geneva.

Golden rule number one

Keep calm and don't panic.

is for Bargaining

And the rules of the game

Due process

Bargaining is inevitable in most cases because most cases are not black or white. The revenue's main aim is to ensure that taxpayers pay the right amount of tax. But what is the right amount of tax is open to discussion.

It should, however, be a discussion and not an argument. The taxpayer's professional adviser has to come up with sound reasons why their client's position is the right one. The revenue has a naturally sceptical view.

At the end of the day, the revenue is also influenced by the total conduct of the case – by the quality of the taxpayer's disclosure and by the co-operation that they receive during their investigation. Good conduct of a case can only reflect in the taxpayer's favour.

Negotiation starts at the very beginning of the process. The adviser contacts the revenue – on a 'no-names' basis if the approach by the taxpayer is a voluntary one – to discuss the terms and scope of the inquiry and the code of practice under which it is to be handled.

'Cases of suspected serious fraud' are pursued under the revenue's Code of Practice 9; other (less serious) cases follow Code of Practice 8. The revenue's position on Code of Practice 9 is laid down in what is known as the Hansard Rules (see below).

It is unhelpful at this stage if your advisers represent a case in a certain way – in order to get off a prosecution or in order to move it from Code 9 to Code 8 – and then the facts subsequently make it obvious that the adviser should have known that the case was more serious. The revenue will not be amused.

Hansard Rules

In answer to a parliamentary question in 1990, the chancellor of the exchequer confirmed long-standing rules on the revenue's bargaining powers in cases of tax fraud. He made three points, known as the Hansard Rules (named after the official published report of British parliamentary proceedings):

1.   The Inland Revenue may accept a **money settlement** instead of instituting criminal proceedings

in cases where fraud is alleged to have been committed by a taxpayer.

2. The revenue can give no undertaking that it will accept such a settlement even if the case is one in which the taxpayer has made a full confession and has fully co-operated in the investigation of the facts. The revenue has **full discretion** in all cases as to the course it pursues.

3. In considering whether to accept a money settlement or to institute criminal proceedings, however, the revenue is influenced by the taxpayer making a **full confession** and fully co-operating in the investigation – by, for instance, allowing the revenue to examine whatever books, papers or documents that they see fit.

In practice, this means that as long as the taxpayer is up-front with the revenue during the process, he or she can be assured that the settlement will remain confidential and will be a civil one. There will be no recourse to criminal law.

The revenue's powers are unique in this respect and differ greatly from those of HM Customs & Excise, for example, and of the police.

Foreign bodies

Anyone sitting offshore (outside the UK's jurisdiction) with no assets whatsoever in this country is faced with a different type of negotiation. The tactic can be 'Come

and get me if you want me', and they can either agree to settle at a certain figure with the revenue or not. In some cases, however, the revenue chooses not to settle on grounds of public policy.

There are a number of people who have settled satisfactorily with the revenue and come back to the UK. But there are also a number who are still living in different jurisdictions and who, to their frustration, have been unable to reach an agreement with the revenue.

Revenue officers

You are not bargaining with a wall. The special compliance officers are considerate and intelligent. They try to be non-confrontational, and it's very easy to relax when being interviewed by them. After ten minutes or so under such conditions you may well be happy to chatter away at will. It's not like being questioned by a uniformed officer. So be careful!

The officers are not unduly bureaucratic. But behind them there is a civil service with rules and regulations. And there are public policy criteria. It's not the Wild West. Which makes it completely different from those jurisdictions where someone's tax affairs can be settled over a good lunch.

On the other hand, it is not the revenue's general policy to bankrupt people. They want them to carry on in business … and to pay their dues.

Don't complain

A lot of people think it's a good idea to threaten to complain about the revenue to a 'higher authority'. They're usually wrong.

There are, of course, standard complaints procedures, and it is possible to go to more senior officials, and even to the ombudsman (called the 'adjudicator'). But to use these procedures tactically just doesn't work. There have to be very genuine reasons for complaint before you can hope to follow that route successfully.

is for Confidentiality

And how much of it you can expect

The revenue are (justly) proud of their record on confidentiality. They understand the real world and that people in it have complex, financial, commercial and personal lives. They go to great lengths to protect confidences and embarrassments.

This means in practice that disclosures can be made on a managed basis. Two spouses, say, can go through one joint disclosure as appropriate, and then have separate meetings with the revenue in which they can make disclosures of which the other will be unaware. Likewise, directors of a business can make disclosures of which fellow directors will remain ignorant.

The revenue is governed by the Official Secrets Act, and certain high-profile people and cases are dealt with on an even stricter regime. There are cases where issues of national security are involved and the details do not even go into the revenue's own computers.

The revenue do, however, have a number of obligations to share information with HM Customs & Excise and with the police.

The revenue lay down their rules on confidentiality in Code of Practice II. In short, they will only give information to people not authorised by the taxpayer in the very restricted cases where it is allowed by law.

The Code specifically says, 'You do not have to discuss your personal tax affairs in front of other people.'

Professional privilege

Whatever you disclose to your lawyer is privileged. It is considered to be as if you are talking to yourself. And since you cannot be forced to reveal your own innermost thoughts to anybody, you cannot be forced to disclose confidences to your lawyer. What you reveal to your tax adviser is also covered by the law on privilege, but less so.

Not everything that you reveal to your lawyer, however, is privileged. For example:

- Original documents recording a transaction are never covered.
- Any communication intended to facilitate a crime is excluded.

- Documents that get into the hands of a third party are usually no longer privileged.

The law on privilege is not clear-cut, though, and you should always ask your adviser what disclosures are covered and what are not. As a result of a recent case, the law now seems to be that a formal notice under section 20(i) of the Taxes Management Act imposes a duty on taxpayers to produce communications with their lawyers.

D

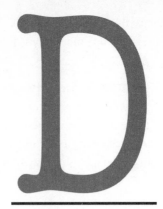

is for Denial

And how to recognise it

Many people's first reaction on hearing that they are under investigation by the Inland Revenue is to go into total denial. 'It wasn't me,' they claim.

This is not a good idea.

One taxpayer told the revenue that he was absolutely squeaky clean. He knew, he said, because he had taken counsel's opinion, and leading counsel had said that everything was okay. As it turned out, everything wasn't okay. Both the taxpayer and counsel ended up in jail.

Lord Denning once said: 'Ignorance is a misfortune, not a privilege, where the law is concerned.'

The style of denial

Denial comes in many forms. Variations that we've heard include:

- It happened in the basement. I never go into the basement.
- Just let me speak to them.
- I've got absolutely nothing to hide.
- I've got no time for this.
- They can do their worst. They'll never find anything.
- I've always had an accountant who's told me it's okay.
- It's a bluff. It's just a fishing expedition.
- Me. I'm squeaky clean.

The last of these is a particular favourite of really hard-

ened fraudsters. But each one can be a leading indicator of serious fiddling.

You can often tell that someone is in denial by their shifty-eyed twitching and fierce determination not to look you straight in the eye. (See 'L is for Languages' for more hints on body language.)

Avoidance versus evasion

Some people go into denial by telling themselves that what they did was to avoid tax legally, not to evade tax illegally. This is a slippery slope. Some of the greatest minds in the land have taxed themselves over the distinction between avoidance and evasion. And still it's not clear.

Tax avoidance is what you do when you stick to the letter, but not the spirit, of the law. Reducing your tax to a minimum whilst sticking to the spirit of the law is called 'tax mitigation', and no one objects to that. By creating things like National Savings certificates, the government in some cases positively encourages it.

But creating artificial devices purely for the purpose of avoiding tax is objectionable and can get you into trouble. The distinction is a fine one and rests on interpreting the intention of parliament when the law was being drafted.

Tax evasion is more straightforward. It involves an undeniable liability to tax and some sort of dishonesty – especially non-disclosure of relevant facts – in the evasion of it. Guilt or innocence turns on a jury's judgement of what constitutes dishonesty.

If you think what you're doing is merely mitigation, check it out with your tax advisers. Otherwise it can all too easily end in litigation.

is for Excuses

Our all-time favourites

Everybody does it…(pause)…don't they?

Do you call this a living?

I didn't gain from it personally.

I was ill, I had a nervous breakdown.

I always wanted to repay it.

I didn't think it was a lot of money…in those days.

I met this chap on a plane and he said it was alright.

I was ridiculed at the golf club because I didn't do it.

It's offshore so I thought it would be okay.

Somebody advised me to do it. I can't remember who. (Or, he's dead now.)

I won it on the horses.

It was a gift.

I thought they'd never find it.

I had a handicapped child/sick relative that I was worried about

It's not that serious…(long pause)…is it?

You think that's my only problem? I've also got the Serious Fraud Office breathing down my neck.

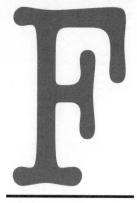

is for Fishing

What tax inspectors do in their spare time

On occasions, tax inspectors seem to set out on fishing expeditions. They ask taxpayers a number of judiciously phrased questions in order to see whether there is a case to be answered.

Sometimes these expeditions lead them to look closely at whole industries. In recent years, for instance, they have looked long and hard at the amusement-arcade business, construction, betting and gaming, commodities dealing, and some doctors and dentists.

Their fishing expeditions have even taken them into the fishing industry.

Inspectors inspecting

The revenue do not just sit around waiting for titbits to fall into their laps. They also go out and search for information. Nowadays, for instance, quite a few inspectors surf the Net in their quieter moments.

Remember also that tax inspectors have spare time, and in it they may do any of the following:

- Drive up and down wealthy residential areas.
- Spend time looking at nice houses, especially expensively renovated ones.
- Drink in pubs and eat in restaurants, taking an exceptional interest in the business's cost structure.

- Cut up newspapers and use the services of press-cutting agencies.
- Access company databases and on-line records from Companies House.
- Check up on local authority parking permits in certain areas.
- Scour the land registry.
- Take holidays abroad.

Information technology

Ultimately, the revenue puts all the information that it gathers into its computers. A tremendous amount of information goes into these computers these days – from the yachting register and airlines' databases to bank account details. And all these sources of data are cross-correlated with each other.

Information technology has worked enormously in the revenue's favour. They have far more sophisticated IT resources than the average business owner can imagine. And they have a skilled project team looking specifically at the uses of IT for tax investigations.

Moreover, they and their computers have long memories. They hold records, some of which go back as far as the 1950s.

is for Goals

And how to score them

The ultimate objective in any negotiation with the revenue is to end up:

(1) with a settlement
(2) without a prosecution.

This clears up the past and puts the taxpayer's affairs straight for the future.

A settlement involves compromise which is, by definition, something that leaves both sides unhappy. If your advisers have done well, you will be less unhappy with the settlement than the revenue.

The goal, as in any A–Z, is to get to Zzzzz … and a good night's sleep.

is for Help
And where to find it

It is not just professional advisers who advise people to seek professional advice. In its own literature, the Inland Revenue says: 'You are advised to seek professional assistance to help you deal with matters raised by the SCO.' The revenue are not vindictive; they appreciate that people are entitled to proper advice.

It is important to get the right sort of advice, which means turning to experienced people. Knowing the statute is not enough. It's a question of knowing how to manage the whole scenario and the players in it. In this, help from the wrong people becomes a hindrance. Don't seek advice in the pub. Friends of friends are not helpful.

This is a niche area and highly specialised, and there are immense pitfalls. If there is a serious possibility of prosecution then you must find a solicitor well versed in dealing with special compliance.

Golden rule number two

Get expert advice. It's always the cheaper option.

Keeping mum

Until you find the right advice, say absolutely nothing – not even 'Good morning' or 'Nice to see you'. It's

astounding how people chatter on when they don't have to. The extent to which people will volunteer information – and quite unnecessarily put themselves in it when putting what they think is the best gloss on things – is quite extraordinary.

Popular opening gambits from those seeking help:

- I was discussing this in the pub, and they said I might have a little problem.
- I was in the golf club and they all laughed. Then I knew it was serious.
- Will they take £50,000 and go away?
- You've got to sort this for me. Just sort it. And now.
- I've got this horrendous problem with the revenue. (This is a minor PAYE matter.)
- I think I've got a little problem. (Those are the mega-cases.)

First steps

The adviser's first step is to place the problem in one of two categories:

1. If it's fairly clear that it is a matter of a monetary settlement only, then the adviser sets out to agree the parameters of the case with the revenue.
2. On the other hand, if the person under investigation is either:
   – a professional person

- someone who has been the subject of a previous inquiry or
- a part of a major conspiracy to defraud

the first decision has to be whether that person needs to see a lawyer.

Lawyers can be on hand very quickly. They can be in your office the same morning; they can be in a hotel near Heathrow that night. Should you wish to stay outside the Inland Revenue's jurisdiction, lawyers can fly out to a meeting on the next available plane. Only on rare occasions are meetings with lawyers difficult to arrange – at times, for example, when the taxpayer is already incarcerated abroad.

is for Information

And the amazing capacity of human beings to grass on each other

Like it or not, we live in a society of informers. The capacity of people to tell tales about each other is limitless. They have a variety of motives – jealousy, envy and hatred being foremost among them – but sometimes their informing is gratuitous. The amount of information that pours into the revenue in this way is staggering.

Informers are often aggrieved spouses or employees, competitors, jealous neighbours, jilted lovers, etc. But there are plenty of other sources of information. Tax inspectors play golf, visit pubs and go to other places frequented by chatterboxes.

They also read newspapers' gossip columns and 'rich lists'. Reading the national and local press wearing a tax inspector's spectacles can be quite a spectacle. It's amazing what you can find out. Stories of lavish parties, drugs, high life styles and large pay-offs can all hint at investigations to come.

The price of martyrdom is not cheap

People don't have to inform on others. The revenue actually respect people who don't give them other peoples' names … but the price of such martyrdom is not always cheap.

Chinese whispers

Gossip is particularly dangerous since it can easily be distorted, like in a game of Chinese whispers.

Aggrieved employees, for instance, might have got hold of only one part of a story when they decide to call the revenue. But once the revenue has been contacted they are sure to follow the contact up. Informers' letters, even if anonymous, stay on file.

There's nothing worse than having the revenue think that something untoward is happening when it isn't. An informer once told them that someone was being paid in 'antique guns'. It took ages to convince them that the guns in question were actually worth no more than £50.

Section 20

The revenue have sweeping powers to demand documents from the taxpayer and from third parties under section 20 or section 745 of the Taxes Management Act. They are always entitled to obtain pieces of paper under a notice if the notice is valid. And they can go back 20 years into a person's affairs in cases of suspected fraud.

What they are not entitled to do is to insist upon an

Golden rule number three

Don't discuss your tax affairs with anyone but a tight circle of professional advisers.

interview with the taxpayer or third parties. They cannot force people to speak.

The revenue are allowed to search premises and remove documents if they have a warrant. If they raid your premises, don't obstruct them. But do follow a few simple rules:

- Make sure your professional adviser gets round to the premises as fast as possible.
- Read the warrant and make sure that you understand it.
- Remember you are under no legal obligation to talk.
- Make sure also that your staff are aware they are under no legal obligation to talk.

- Ask what is the purpose of the search.
- Obtain a receipt for any materials that they take away.
- Get the name and office of the investigator in charge.

is for Jail

And when you get to go there

In practice, the revenue prosecute very rarely. So the number of investigations that end up with someone in prison is relatively small. It does, however, include some famous names – Lester Piggott, for example, and (in the United States) Al Capone.

The sentences given by judges are often far more severe than the average person in the street would imagine for the level of the offence. In 1998 someone was jailed for 15 months for fraud involving less than £100,000. Sentencing is not always consistent either. Someone else went to jail for just 12 months for a £500,000 fraud.

If the revenue say they are going to prosecute, the

consequences can be very serious. You must seek professional advice immediately. There is no alternative.

Even if you are acquitted, the trauma of a trial is punishment enough.

Each year, the revenue initiates over 100 criminal proceedings.
Between 10 and 25 cases relate to false accounts or false claims.
Two thirds of these cases result in a conviction.

There are five simple ways to avoid going to jail:

- Don't lie to the revenue.
- Don't lie to the revenue.
- Don't lie to the revenue.
- Don't lie to the revenue.
- Don't lie to the revenue.

Golden rule number four

Don't lie to the revenue.

You can't go to jail unless you're prosecuted. And some people are more likely to be prosecuted than others. For example:

- Professional people – lawyers, accountants, etc.
- Anyone who is part of a conspiracy, someone who has been manufacturing invoices, for instance.
- People who have already been investigated by the revenue. Although the revenue will never guarantee it, there is a very high chance that you will not go to jail for a first offence if your case is handled correctly.
- People whose headed paper incorporates words like Cayman, Liberia, Vanuatu or Andorra.

K

is for Knowledge

And how much more of it the revenue have than you

As in a game of poker, the revenue keep their cards close to their chest. You never quite know what they know.

The amount varies in different cases. Sometimes their knowledge is excellent, but they can't use it. They know the end, but they haven't quite got there yet.

On the other hand, sometimes (though rarely) they're just fishing.

And sometimes their information is totally incorrect.

Golden rule number five

Don't assume that the revenue are ignorant of anything.

Sources

Although the revenue get a lot of their information from informers and gossip (see 'I is for Information'), they have additional (and more formal) sources. For example: there are lists of the owners of private planes and of classic cars, and of the customers of firms of specialist suppliers, like the builders of swimming pools.

The revenue have access to the passenger lists of all airlines flying scheduled flights in and out of UK airports over the past ten years. They look at suspects' houses, holiday homes, school fees and charitable giving. On occasions, they use the government chemist and handwriting analysts. And soon there will be links between the revenue's databases and those of the DSS and HM Customs & Excise.

is for Languages
And what they can tell you

People often underestimate the inspectors' knowledge of foreign languages. Some of them speak two or three – including ones that you might not expect: Russian, Chinese, Polish, Danish and various Indian dialects, for example.

With the opening up of the revenue as an equal opportunities employer, a number of inspectors from a variety of ethnic groups (and with an array of language skills) have risen to high places. In any case, the revenue have never hesitated to call in interpreters.

The revenue are also highly skilled at understanding unspoken languages – the way that letters are constructed, for instance, or the body language of people attending meetings.

These skills can be turned the other way round. For example, it is sometimes possible to gauge where inspectors are coming from by the way that their letters are constructed and from the tone of their questioning.

But this is not infallible. One expensive visit to leading counsel to seek an opinion on what a rather strangely worded letter from the revenue meant, turned out to be a complete waste of money. Only later did it transpire that the letter had in fact been written in a great hurry late one Friday afternoon in order to comply with a 28-day rule on replies that was in operation at the time. The (fairly junior) writer had been in such a hurry that he had not been able to find a senior person to clear the letter.

Revenue speak

The revenue have a language all their own. Among their most common phrases and sayings are:

- There may be very serious consequences. (This means: We might well prosecute.)
- We are disappointed with your report. (There is a significant omission.)
- Shouldn't you have another word with your client? (We really do have something on him.)
- This disclosure is not complete. (You've missed out a bank account.)
- Is there anything else? (I'm fishing.)
- Can I come and see you? (If not, I'll serve a section 20 notice and might even raid you anyway.)

Taxpayer speak

Taxpayers also have their own language:

- I can't remember. (Advisers could spend all day listening to their clients repeat 'I can't remember'.)
- Tell them they can go and rot in hell. (I really want to settle urgently.)
- I don't care if this thing drags on for years. (If you don't settle within seven days I'm going to have a heart attack.)
- Do you remember everything that I tell you? (I've said more than I wanted to.)
- Somebody told me that it happened to him. (I'm telling you the truth now.)
- I've never done nothing. (I've done lots.)
- I'm totally innocent. (I'm guilty as hell.)

Hypothetically speaking

There is a wonderful word in the English language – 'hypothetically'. Hypothetically means that what follows is exactly what I've done. For example, 'Hypothetically, I could have been putting all that into a Swiss bank account.' 'Hypothetically, my brother-in-law could have been the trustee.'

Body language

The revenue are skilled at reading body language. There are usually two inspectors at any interview with a tax-payer, and one of them is watching the body language.

There has been talk about video-taping sessions and then speeding up the video because that accentuates body language. But that has not been introduced yet. In any case, the revenue would not record or video something without everybody knowing that it was taking place.

M

is for Meetings

And how to behave in them

Meetings with both the revenue and the taxpayer present are tense and best avoided.

In Code 8 cases there is usually no need for the client to meet the revenue. But in Code 9 cases they usually have to meet at least twice – once in a formal interview and once again at the final settlement. There are exceptions in the case of ill health or age, or if the person is outside the jurisdiction (i.e. if they've done a bunk).

Invariably, taxpayers themselves want to see the revenue. Their approach is: 'I'll see them and I'll sort it'. But taxpayers are usually bad in meetings. They're embarrassed to say 'I don't know', so they start babbling, guessing and then they trip up.

Meetings without the client present are carried on in a more professional way. There is less emotion in the air.

Comfort time

So-called 'comfort breaks' are allowed in meetings. The number of trips per hour taken by clients to the toilet in such meetings is at least double the national average.

Golden rule number six

Be well prepared for meetings. People don't plan to fail; they fail to plan.

Rules for meetings

1. Dress down, leave your diamonds and the Jaeger le Coultre at home. The more natural you look and behave, the better you come across.

2. Don't hold meetings in the revenue's own offices; it's far too intimidating. Opt for your adviser's office. There are even occasions when holding meetings in your own home can be advantageous. The revenue are going to have a good look at the home anyway. But if they come, make sure that the rest of the family is out for the day.

3. If you get kicked under the table by your adviser, don't ask: 'Why are you kicking me?'

4. Don't rejoice too soon. One taxpayer came out of a meeting in London's High Holborn and jumped for joy in the street outside – not realising that the inspector was looking at him from an upstairs window. He went straight from High Holborn to Deep Water.

5. The better prepared you are, the better the outcome. People who just run straight into meetings generally come unstuck. They tend to make guesses when under pressure, out of a tremendous urge to give an answer to questions. This can lead to real problems when the true picture becomes known later.

Nota bene

The revenue always take excellent notes of meetings and it can be quite shocking when someone starts to read out very precise notes of what you said nine months earlier.

You have a right to see the notes, but you have to ask for them. The revenue will want them to be signed and returned with a record of any disagreement or amendment.

There are no hidden tape recorders in meetings. The revenue will always tell you in advance if they wish to tape a conversation.

N

is for Neglect

And how not to

Neglect used to be a good idea – carry on long enough and the inspector retires (see under 'T is for Time') or gets promoted to higher things. But this is not the case today. Now it's far better to get matters out of the way – if only for your peace of mind.

Wilful neglect is something else – and you can actually be penalised for it. When does neglect become wilful? It's a matter of interpretation, but most people recognise wilfulness when they see it.

is for Overseas

Where people tend to think that assets are safe

For a tax inspector, the word 'overseas' is like a red rag to a bull. Whenever there is an overseas element (like an offshore trust, foreign income or an overseas residence) the revenue look at the case more closely. They assume that the main reason for anyone to have money offshore is to avoid tax.

They also have a general belief that if they shake any offshore structure hard enough, money will fall into their laps. And it often does.

Cases like Robert Maxwell's increase the scrutiny of parliament and of the revenue into offshore structures. And they tend to lead to legislation that shuts loopholes

in later years. Tax avoidance in its sophisticated form is not popular with the electorate of this country.

People think that as long as their money is offshore, nothing will happen to it. But that is not the case. Over time they become lax. They start to bring it home in cash to pay caterers and swimming-pool makers – and then they throw big parties that make it into the local papers. Few stick to the letter of the advice they have been given.

No secrets

The IT revolution and the growth of international treaties have dented the idea that somewhere there is complete secrecy allied with complete safety. Tax havens, including places like Switzerland, are increasingly having their secrecy breached.

In one case, a customs officer on the French/Italian border impounded a banker's briefcase. In it was a list of French customers' bank accounts in Switzerland – a list that was passed over to the French tax authorities.

Some people believe that they are going to be able to settle more satisfactorily if they are outside the revenue's jurisdiction, notwithstanding the revenue's statements to the contrary. But they have to be prepared for a prolonged six- or seven-year battle. It takes much longer to get information when overseas jurisdictions are involved.

Some people become non-resident in order to avoid tax, and then subsequently come to regret it. They end up settling with the revenue just in order to return to England.

There are some offshore residents, however, who have been prepared to settle for significant sums of money but have found that the revenue have refused their offer and continued to prosecute.

Nobody, though, has yet been extradited to the UK for tax fraud alone. But there is growing international pressure to move tax evasion into the same category as other fraud and white-collar crime.

is for Penalties

And how steep they can be

People tend to worry about penalties too early. They start by saying "I've got £500,000 that I haven't paid tax on. How much will it cost me?" In the first instance, if they say £500,000 then it's probably over £2 million. The key thing, however, is not the penalty but the amount of tax to be paid. Even though the penalties can theoretically be as high as 100% of the unpaid tax, in practice they are nearly always dwarfed by the amount of tax to be paid.

If you can bring the tax figure down, you get a lower interest figure too (since that is statutorily determined) – whilst another 5% or 10% off the penalty doesn't materially affect most settlements. Note that penalties are imposed on the tax only, not on the interest.

Penalties are reduced for good behaviour.

- The revenue give up to 30% for **full and early disclosure**;
- They give up to 40% for **full co-operation** during the investigation;
- They can give over 30% based on the **relative (un)seriousness** of the case.

On top of that, there is the apocryphal story about the Scottish tax inspector who offered an extra 5% to a UK-resident German whose children had been educated in Scottish schools and who had Scottish accents. The German tax authorities, on the other hand, are understood to be totally unmoved by Scottish accents.

Golden rule number seven

Make significant payments on account. There is no better sign of co-operation with the revenue.

Three ways of dealing with penalties:

Focus on mitigating the tax.
Focus on mitigating the tax.
Focus on mitigating the tax.

If there's a draw (i.e., both sides end up equally unhappy), then there may be a victory to be won on penalties in the final shoot-out.

is for Questions

And who gets to ask what, of whom

The revenue's powers are limited to demanding and obtaining pieces of paper – and that includes electronic data. There is no obligation on anyone to say anything at any time.

However, people have an incredible desire to answer questions that they were never asked. When the revenue turn up on the doorstep with their ID cards to ask questions about a third party, they frequently get answers that any agony aunt or psychiatrist would be proud of.

Third parties usually start to co-operate as soon as it's clear that their affairs are not being investigated.

Quite often they'll add a bit. 'I know you're here about Mr Smith. But wouldn't you like to hear about Mr Brown? It's the same thing.'

This involuntary ratting is not necessarily done with malice. It just makes people feel important. They can then tell their friends: 'I was talking to the revenue today.'

All correct and complete?

In Code 9 cases, where serious fraud is suspected, the revenue will hand you a schedule of five formal questions. These are:

(1) Have you omitted or incorrectly recorded any transactions in the books of any business with which you have been connected?

(2) To the best of your knowledge, are all these books correct and complete?

(3) Are the tax returns of all these businesses correct and complete?

(4) Are your personal tax returns also correct and complete?

(5) Will you allow the revenue to examine your business records, bank statements and personal financial records to check that you've given the correct answers to questions 1–4?

Before you answer, you will be advised that the questions:

- have no time limit
- cover the tax history of all businesses that you have been involved with
- relate to your current knowledge, not the knowledge you had when you submitted your tax returns
- can be answered by 'yes' or 'no'
- deserve serious thought, and
- are considered to be reasonable by the courts.

The reason for the outpouring of guilt – often from innocent people – is much the same as that which leads the innocent to twitch when they pass through customs, whilst the guilty (revealingly) play it straight.

Q & A

'What's your name?'
'Smith', should be the answer.

But most people say something like:

'My name is Tommy Smith and I live in Lancaster and I went on holiday last year with my wife and kids. And do you know where we went? Here, here are the photographs. And I've got a mother-in-law and I've got a bit of trouble with the mother-in-law, so we decided to take her on holiday with us. And then I met this fellow on the plane. And he gave me this slip of paper to fill out, and he charged me £5,000 and asked if I could pay him in cash. And then he said that as my mother-in-law was not domiciled, if she paid it into his Swiss bank account there'd be no VAT. But I thought it was just the VAT. I didn't know it was anything to do with the revenue.'

Always assume that every question has a purpose. Even asking your name.

- 'Where did you go for your holidays this year?' means 'How did you pay for them?'
- 'Are you not feeling well?' means 'Have you got medical insurance?'

-      'Where do your children go to school?' means 'How many sets of school fees are you paying?'

The revenue are not shy about asking for money, and about asking for it now. They have, however, been known to decline a payment on account. But that is very rare, and very recent. When it occurs, it is because they consider the amount to be insulting. It doesn't help the conduct of the case when a payment is returned.

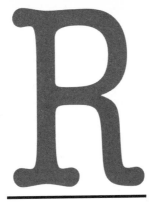

is for Remorse

And when it's too late

Most taxpayers have regrets immediately after a settlement. Invariably they think that (with, of course, better help from their advisers) they could have got away with less. It's amazing how small a problem seems once it's been solved.

People in remorse tend to want to talk it out. But if you're under investigation you should talk about the case only to your advisers and (maybe) to your co-directors or spouses (but see 'W is for Weekends'). The more you offload your woes on to another person, the more that person in turn needs to offload them on to someone else.

In one case, a taxpayer told the revenue that £250,000 was the absolute limit to what he could afford. But then he boasted around town that he was

going to settle for £500,000, '…and it'll be a really good deal'. Unfortunately for him, two of the people he told about his really good deal later gave evidence to the revenue about what he had said. His big mouth left him with a big bill.

Remorse and self-pity are wholly counterproductive. The more that people can put the emotion of the issue to one side and (assuming that there is no risk of prosecution) treat the case on businesslike lines, the more satisfactory will be the outcome. It wastes an awful lot of time having to repeat 'Isn't it terrible?' and 'Woe is me'.

Fire and flood

It's a rare case that does not involve a fire or flood in which the only thing that gets damaged is the actual room, filing cabinet or drawer where the key documents are housed. The evidence is invariably there. The documents are indeed sopping wet. But the priceless stamp collection in the drawer below is somehow left miraculously untouched.

And it is truly amazing how often major removal firms in this country are alleged to have lost accounting and tax records whilst absolutely everything else – including the most delicate works of art – have remained totally unscathed.

Anyone who goes into this business sooner or later becomes a believer in miracles.

Golden rule number eight

Don't try to destroy evidence. It's usually unhelpful.

Any pub within half a mile of an Inland Revenue office is a no-go area. There is always the possibility that inspectors are having an internal review meeting at one and the same time as a suspect is giving high fives all round.

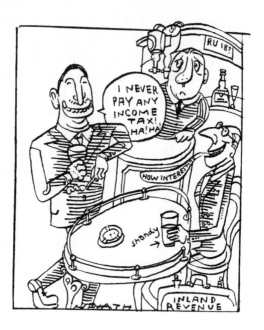

S

is for Solutions

Know where you're going and you might just get there

As early in the process as possible, work out a strategy and decide on what a reasonable settlement is likely to be. That may have to be modified as information becomes available during the process. But if you are able to see the end at the beginning then you're better able to work towards it.

In a lot of cases, an adviser can tell in the first hour of the first meeting how the case will progress. They cannot forecast the actual outcome, but they do know the parameters of the negotiation.

The bigger cases are more difficult. Here a controlled management process is necessary. Advisers need to sit down and form a plan in consultation with their clients, and also with the revenue. Sharing a problem with the revenue can be helpful. They are always prepared to listen to lateral thinking.

Planning the process and knowing where you're going saves money – in terms of both tax and advisers' fees. A lot of money can be wasted doing work in irrelevant areas.

is for Time

And how long the whole thing takes

The duration of an investigation varies according to the availability of information, the temperament of the players, and the speed with which the revenue can review the adviser's report on the case. An adviser should be able to give a rough timetable at a fairly early stage. The usual time is 6–12 months.

Every case is different, but the diagram on pages 66–67 gives some idea of the steps that typically have to be taken.

It is a disappointment if a case – from beginning to end – has not been cleared within 18 months. With a technically based case, however, it can take much longer – if, for example, both sides need to seek tax counsel's advice. When parts have to be taken to the Commissioners, a case can stretch for years.

From start to finish – a typical investigation

Notification letter from the SCO or voluntary disclosure
An investigation is prompted either when the SCO believes it has a case to pursue or if you volunteer information to the revenue.

Appointment of advisers
Before you do anything else, appoint a team of professional advisers.

Initial meeting with the SCO
Your advisers will meet the SCO to assess the seriousness of the case.

Code 9 or Code 8 investigation
Code 9 means you are under investigation for fraud. A Code 8 investigation involves other forms of non-payment.

Formal interview
Also known as the 'Hansard meeting', the interview is based on 5 key questions. Attended by you, the SCO and your advisers.

Scoping meeting
Your advisers will meet the SCO again, this time to discuss the scope of the investigation.

Preparation and submission of the report
Prepared by your adviser, the report represents your case to the SCO.

Clarification meeting
The SCO may wish to meet your advisers to discuss outstanding queries. Usually marks the start of settlement negotiations.

Settlement meeting
The conclusion of settlement negotiations. The SCO invites you to offer a settlement. Usually a formality unless there are still issues to resolve.

Letter of offer
A formal letter to the SCO, prepared by your advisers and signed by you.

Formal acceptance
The SCO reply in due course, confirming their acceptance of the offer.

Slow down

There are cases where it can be of benefit to delay.

Delaying tactics used to be used more often. It was thought that they increased the chances of a reasonable settlement, on the grounds that after a case had dragged on for years some inspector somewhere would eventually decide that it had to be resolved – just to get it off the books.

But times have changed. The investigation process is becoming more sophisticated. And fairer.

In general, more people want to reduce the length of an investigation than to prolong it. Typical attitudes are:

- '1 want it sorted … now.'
- 'I'm paying you money. Get it fixed. And fast.'
- 'If I pay them £50,000, tell them to get off my back.' £50,000 seems to be the standard opening figure in any case where settlement should be in excess of £1 million.

is for Underestimate

And when not to

At the beginning of every case, the revenue always grossly overestimate the amount that's in it for them, and taxpayers always grossly underestimate the amount for which they can settle. As a general rule, add a nought to your estimate (so £50,000 becomes £500,000), and knock a nought off the revenue's figure ('millions' becomes 'hundreds of thousands').

These incompatible expectations are the main reason why neither party is ever happy with the settlement that they reach.

Serious consequences

'Serious consequences' is a favourite phrase of the revenue. They're not allowed to say 'prosecution', so they use 'serious consequences' as an alternative. 'There could be very serious consequences arising from this' means, 'We haven't got enough on you to prosecute – yet'.

The phrase is used to such an extent that the letters 'SCO' have sometimes been thought to stand for the Serious Consequences Office. Among advisers, there is a competition to find the inspector who says 'serious consequences' the most times in one hour.

Never underestimate

- The revenue's estimation of you. They know that the people they are investigating are clever and sophisticated. If they weren't, they wouldn't be where they are.
- The ability of the revenue to use sophisticated information technology.
- The revenue's skill at playing games of bluff.

is for Volunteers

And how they get the better deals

There are two things to remember about volunteering information:

1.   If you do it, you'll get a better deal. You'll pay less money (see 'P is for Penalties') and you'll also be treated in a less aggressive way. You've done the revenue's work for them, so they'll naturally feel more warmly towards you.

2.   Never volunteer a partial disclosure. Many people make the mistake of thinking that they can volunteer 60% of the missing money and get away with the rest. But if that's what they want to do, they are better off not going down the disclosure route at all. The Inland Revenue have a duty to

Golden rule number nine

Don't suffer from selective amnesia when disclosing information voluntarily.

check everything anyway. They're bound to look into the things that you don't tell them. Incomplete disclosure, especially under Code of Practice 9, is likely to lead to 'serious consequences'.

Market forces

Volunteers became more numerous after the USM (the Unlisted Securities Market) came into being in the 1980s. It enabled entrepreneurs to sell their businesses for several times the value of their company's annual earnings, and it did not take a doctorate in mathematics to work out that this was better (financially as well as morally) than sticking a hand in the till. Not only did capitalism make entrepreneurs better off, it also made them more honest.

Before they could sell their company in this way, however, many entrepreneurs had to clean it up. Some took the decision to clean up slowly over time, and then to sell after the statutory disclosure periods had passed. Others took the decision to go to the revenue immediately, come clean, and then sell. That pattern has continued with the growth of other junior stock markets over the years and the increased availability of venture capital.

is for Weekends

And how to manage family, friends
and the rest of your life

The most stressful events in life are said to be divorce, the death of a partner and moving house. Coming under investigation by the Inland Revenue does not fall far below them.

The vast majority of investigations involve prolonged and stressful negotiations between the person under investigation, their advisers, and the Inland Revenue. Investigations last for 6–12 months (if you're lucky) and in that time they are bound to affect relationships.

Hints on how to manage stress – 1

- Keep your business going as usual.
- Keep it clean.
- Maintain your normal life as far as possible.
- Don't go travelling excessively, but do take a holiday.
- Don't go shopping excessively.
- Take regular physical exercise, or use any natural means of relaxation. (Pills are rarely a good idea.)

If you are ill, produce a doctor's certificate to that effect. The revenue are not unsympathetic to ill health. They won't interrogate someone who is elderly and frail – which does not mean that they won't investigate them. Ill health is not a bar to considering a case for prosecution.

Hints on how to manage stress – 2

Some people turn to prayer. And if it makes them feel better, and better able to get a grip on things, then it's a good thing.

But if you feel moved to charity, deeds of covenant or gift aid are recommended for all charitable giving, including gifts to the church. Don't make the mistake of one businessman whose donations to charity exceeded his declared income. That can take a bit of explaining.

Hints on how to manage stress – 3

*   Be careful where you talk. In the early days of mobile phones, people were picking up conversations with scanners and passing on the details to the revenue.
*   Be careful whom you talk to. Don't seek advice at the golf club or try to have meaningful discussions about your case at dinner parties.

On the other hand, it's a rare person who doesn't need someone to talk to, and a strong emotional base when you come home at night is usually helpful. But in a country where long-term relationships are becoming the exception rather than the rule, using your nearest and dearest as an emotional support has to be set against the danger that they will no longer be so near and dear when the revenue come to call.

Never involve children. It doesn't help. They get the wrong angle.

is for Xenophobia

The fear of foreign tax authorities

'Xenophobia' is defined in the dictionary as 'a morbid dislike of foreigners'. Taxpayers have good reason to be morbid about foreign tax authorities these days. For the amount of information coming to the revenue from overseas is on the increase.

New treaties with countries in the former communist bloc, for example, have led to information exchanges with places like Poland. Old treaties, with EU countries and the United States in particular, are being updated all the time.

The revenue also have exchange programmes with inspectors from abroad, and they make reciprocal goodwill visits.

On occasions, they are asked to do an investigation

for an overseas authority. America's tax authority, the IRS, recently paid a visit to some people in Miami and announced, 'We're here at the request of our friends in the UK's Inland Revenue'. Likewise, people in the UK have suddenly found themselves subject to inquiries that have started in offshore jurisdictions.

On one occasion the UK revenue asked a French inspector to look at a particular property in France. When he went to see it, the inspector noted all the cars with British registration plates that happened to visit the house. And that led to an interesting investigation.

Other countries have different structures for investigating fiscal crime. The relationships here with other

authorities – with the DTI, HM Customs & Excise, the police, the Serious Fraud Office, etc. – may not be as close in other countries.

Sometimes treatment elsewhere is less severe, but sometimes it's not. People tend to think that the jurisdiction they're in is the worst – though there is a widespread perception that the United States might be the worst of all.

is for Yarns

Some favourites

The revenue asked a caterer who was being investigated if they could visit his premises. He had time to make one phone call, and when the revenue arrived they found the offices open. But the main kitchens next door were securely padlocked and bolted. The revenue insisted that they be opened, and when they entered they found all the ovens cooking beautifully. There was, however, not a soul to be seen. It was a case of the Marie Celeste.

***

An inspector who was on holiday in Germany took a little detour in order to pay a call on one particular company. When he arrived, the company told him that its headquarters were in London and that London was the main base of its board of directors. They also gave him the address. So when he returned home he paid them a visit. And they told him that the company's head office and main base of its board of directors was (yes, you guessed it) in Germany.

***

In one raid on a taxpayer's house, the revenue, the suspect, his adviser and the police were all sitting round a table when the revenue asked to see some documents. The suspect said he'd go and fetch them. When he hadn't returned 15 minutes later, the revenue realised he'd done a bunk. He'd also locked them all in the room. In fact, he'd taken the documents and got away with them across the roof. The police missed him at Heathrow by about an hour. Needless to say, the documents disappeared. The suspect's associate is at this moment sitting in prison.

***

One man who regularly put cash into an offshore account pleaded that he was so involved with his work that he really didn't pay attention to money. And he certainly didn't have the time to commit tax fraud. So the revenue were rather bemused to find that he did have the time – once a week, in fact – to spend half a day travelling to a bank in order to pay in cash.

***

In the middle of one meeting with the revenue, a taxpayer persuaded them that he needed to take a comfort break in order to remove the brand new Rolls Royce that he'd inadvertently left parked outside the window. It was one of the longest comfort breaks ever taken.

***

After one three-hour meeting in which a lady client sobbed almost continuously, she looked up when the revenue had left and asked her adviser – without a tear to be seen – 'How did I do?'

is for Zzzzzzz…

And rediscovering the meaning of a good night's sleep

Most people under investigation find that all their aches, pains and illnesses disappear, on average, within 30 seconds of reaching a settlement with the revenue.

Experience shows that settlement also has a beneficial effect on the following:

- Sleep
- Sex
- Bank managers
- Pets
- Digestive systems.

Golden rule number ten

Once you've reached a settlement, don't offend again. The revenue does not look kindly on serial evaders.

The
ten golden
rules

Golden rule number one

Keep calm and don't panic.

Golden rule number two

Get expert advice. It's always the cheaper option.

Golden rule number three

Don't discuss your tax affairs with anyone but a
tight circle of professional advisers.

Golden rule number four

Don't lie to the revenue.

Golden rule number five

Don't assume that the revenue is ignorant of anything.

Golden rule number six

Be well prepared for meetings. People don't plan to fail; they fail to plan.

Golden rule number seven

Make significant payments on account. There is no better sign of co-operation with the revenue.

Golden rule number eight

Don't try to destroy evidence. It's usually unhelpful.

Golden rule number nine

Don't suffer from selective amnesia when disclosing information voluntarily.

Golden rule number ten

Once you've reached a settlement, don't offend again. The revenue does not look kindly on serial evaders.